**CAVAN COUNTY ENTERPRISE
BOARD**
17, Farnham Street, Cavan.
Tel. 049-32427
Promoting Student Enterprise

**CAVAN COUNTY ENTERPRISE
BOARD**
17, Farnham Street, Cavan.
Tel. 049-32427
Promoting Student Enterprise

Kevin Kelly

Born in 1966, Kevin Kelly started his career in selling at a young age in the family business in Ballintubber, County Roscommon. In 1987, he graduated from University College Galway with a degree in Commerce.

From 1987 to 1990, he worked in senior management positions in Ireland and England before returning to Ireland to establish his company, *Advanced Marketing*.

One of his major objectives has been to thoroughly research the area of personal excellence. This quest involved spending time at Harvard Business School, and a period at the NLP Practitioner Center in Colorado, where he obtained his Practitioner Accreditation. He has also been awarded EM™ Practitioner Accreditation in Australia.

Since 1990, he has addressed thousands of people. Parents, students, teachers, company directors, sales people, the unemployed and many other groups have benefited from his insights into personal excellence.

He passionately believes that people can live their dreams - if they are willing to take action.

Published 1997 for K. Kelly by On Stream Publications Ltd.,
Cloghroe, Blarney, Co. Cork, Ireland.
Tel/fax: + 353 21 385798
e mail: onstream@indigo.ie

© Kevin Kelly

A CIP record for this book is available from the British Library.

Printed in Ireland by ColourBooks.

The moral right of the author has been asserted.

ISBN: 1 897 685 81 5

HOW?
WHEN YOU
DON'T KNOW
HOW...

KEVIN KELLY

ON STREAM

ACKNOWLEDGEMENTS

A special thanks to the team who constructively criticised the many drafts of this book:

Peter Groves: Thanks a million for your input, energy and enthusiasm. I look forward to contributing to your journey in the future.

Graeme Prevost: For stretching me outside my comfort zone, for the hire of your fantastic analytical mind, thanks from the heart.

Margaret Horan: For your enthusiasm, your stories, your direction and your unconditional support, go raibh míle maith agat.

Jerry Whelan: Your assistance was invaluable - thanks.

Inez Bailey: For your incisive review, and for your ongoing friendship and support - thanks.

Anton Schwarzinger: For your wisdom and your review, thanks. Yes, Anton, "in silence comes wisdom."

Seán McGlynn: For your ideas and enthusiasm, thanks.

Maureen McCann: Thanks for your stories and your inspiration, and for some worldly advice.

Tommy O'Hara: For your objective review and your continued friendship, thanks.

To the rest of the team: **Tom Joyce, Elaine Denby, Pat Campbell, Dick Hinchy, Amanda Campbell, John Mulrennan, Carole Taylor, Fergal McAndrew, Johnny Lynagh, Stephanie O'Connor, Pat Dalton, Dette Kelly** and **Kevin Fahy.**

To my excellent trainers: **Charlie Harrison** and **Jim Sullivan**, who taught me the meaning of self-respect; **Pat Campbell** and **Pat Dalton**, who opened doors for me when I could not find the key, and **Ron Urughart**, whose Vision Quest training was for me a life-changing experience. Thanks a million.

To all the Vision Quest participants, who inspired me to greater heights.

To my friends, who have always supported me in the belief that the impossible was possible, and who were willing to invest in me at an early stage (thanks John).

To my clients, who are invariably my friends, thanks for your trust and your support.

To my excellent support team: my personal assistant, **Eithne Fannon**, who has had to listen to me for the last few years (an art in itself), but who, more importantly, shared the joys and pains of the journey. Thanks a million.

To **Orla McGowan**, who assisted in the Summer of '97. The world is your oyster (that is the easiest prediction I have ever made).

Finally, to my family, who have always been there for me along the way, a sincere thanks.

For more information on Vision Quest, contact them at PO Box 1525, Preston South 3072, Victoria, Australia. Tel: 613-9416-9718.

To my fantastic parents,
who I love dearly:
Kevin Kelly and Mary Kelly.

And to my very special friend,
Veronica Dunne.

PREFACE

Having had the honour of addressing thousands of people on the topic of personal excellence at this stage of my career, I can say without doubt that the most popular question from the audience was "How do I change...how do I improve my lot.?" This book equips you with some of the answers to this question; i.e. the tools for change.

Probably the golden key to a more fulfilling life which, in my opinion has escaped so many for so long, is to look within; to "search for the hero inside;" to tap into the inner power resident in everybody regardless of their background.

Ironically, many of us have tended to look to the external world for our solutions; addictions to things, to drink, to work, to drugs...alas, to find they only yield a temporary buzz.

"The stories of past courage can define that ingredient, they can teach, they can offer hope, they can provide inspiration. But they can't supply courage itself, for this each man must look into his own soul." - John Fitzgerald Kennedy

This book is divided into three sections:

SECTION 1 - THE POTENTIAL

This section highlights the incredible achievements we all record as we go through life, regardless of our circumstances. After reading it, you will realise that you have all the resources required to make your journey a more fulfilling one.

Thus it is now up to you to take control, to take responsibility. None of your past excuses will stand up in the 'court of happiness.'

SECTION 2 - THE PASSAGE

The passage details our journey through life and the inevitable challenges we meet along the way. Each chapter provides the reader with the necessary skills to deal with the ensuing obstacles.

In Chapter 2, the popular dilemma..."not knowing where I am going...I don't know what I want," is discussed. Practically speaking, we *need* to know; ironically, we *do* know. Moreover it is vital that we have a vision to propel us forward.

Often, many people spend their life going forward from goal to goal without fully enjoying the journey. This challenge is discussed in *Carpe Diem*; Chapter 3.

Few reach their chosen destination in the fast lane... doubts, worries, failures are an inevitable part of the journey - Chapter 4.

A side-effect of living in our fast-moving, ever-changing society is that many of us alienate ourselves from our true source of power: The Power Within. Only when we take time out to be silent, to tune into this power, will we find the real map for growth and happiness. This is the focus of Chapter 5.

In Chapter 6, our ability to communicate, the key competency is reviewed. In Chapter 7, the ongoing challenge of dismissing misleading advice from ill-informed people is discussed.

In the final chapter, the focus shifts from 'me' to 'us' as we discuss the critical issue of relationships.

SECTION 3 - THE BOTTOM LINE

This section deals with what must be considered as *The Major Issue*; the bottom line; 'taking action'. I am continually asked what differentiates winners from losers. It is simple: one takes action, the other does not. The people who read this book and take action are the real winners.

As you review this book you will notice many of the following recurring themes:

☀ You have all the resources. You can do it!

☀ Only you can do it to yourself. You cannot change others nor can it be 'done unto you.' *You* have got to make it happen.

"Be the change you want to see in the world." - Gandhi

☀ It is *your* interpretation that counts.
Each of us will, for example, experience failure in our lives; but it is not the experience that is significant, it is how we interpret it. This is why one can assert there is no such thing as reality, only our perception of what reality is.
To some, failure is an excellent learning experience. To others, failure is the signal to throw in the towel. Thus, just like a little child, some get up and try again, others will not.

"The bond of a slave is snapped the moment he considers himself to be a free being." - Gandhi

☀ Be like little children... They live for the moment; their emotions come and go; they are willing to learn; they are totally uninhibited and free from the chains of conditioning. Finally, they know how to have fun...

"If there is anything that we wish to change in the child, we should first examine it and see whether it is not something that could be better changed in ourselves." Carl Jung.

☀ Shape your destiny by declaring your goals to the universe. If they add value to the planet, you will be shown the way, as long as you are 'aware.' Information will come your way packaged as apparent coincidences, intuitions, strange circumstances, declarations from new teachers. Just be 'aware.'

☀ Along the passage take time to 'be;' take time to **rest** that incredible resource that finds no space in this crazy world. Take time to acknowledge and learn from this power within.

☀ Love yourself. It is the key to superior relationships.

☀ Every emotion will come and go if you so choose. Moreover, the more you attach to an unwanted emotion, the more power you give it.

☀ Everything counts! Your words, your physiology, your expectations, have a profound effect on your outcomes.

This book may just be your first step towards a deeper understanding of where you are at in life; on the other hand, applying many of the ideas/tools contained in this publication could bring rewards beyond your wildest dreams. It is a good idea to read the book cover to cover initially; follow this by reviewing it in detail one chapter a day. This review should involve discussing its contents with somebody else. Remember, the best way to learn is to teach others. More importantly, it is essential you dedicate enough time and energy to the exercises (30 minutes daily recommended). You will find that some exercises work better than others; work with what you find most comfortable.

Note: The tools outlined in this publication will only be effective if your primary motivation is to add value to this planet. Those who find pleasure in using these techniques to exploit others, manipulate situations to their benefit, to take even more without ever giving will find pure happiness an elusive goal.

I want you to commit yourself to taking action. "Knowing" and "doing" are poles apart. With knowledge comes responsibility. Once you read this book you disclaim all right to blame, complain and justify why things are the way they are for you - so before we proceed, make the commitment.

I am willing to take the next step, realising that whatever I shall sow, I shall reap.

_____

Signature please.

Remember, knowledge is only useful if used.

Till we meet again,
go for happiness, you deserve it!

Kevin.

CONTENTS

THE POTENTIAL

1. Reigniting The Fire Within   12

THE PASSAGE

2. Going Somewhere or going nowhere   32
3. Carpe Diem...Seize the Day   54
4. Troubled Waters   68
5. In Silence Comes Wisdom   82
6. Do I Know You From Somewhere?...
    the art of building rapport   92
7. Choose Who To Listen To   110
8. To Love Yourself, the start of great relationships   124

THE BOTTOM LINE

9. All Great Achievements Start with one Small Step   136

The Last Word   139
Bibliography   142

1
REIGNITING THE FIRE WITHIN

It is time for an awakening!

By reviewing the many achievements you record in life detailed in this chapter you will realise "Yes, I have the power; yes, I did it before, I can do it again; yes, I have got the potential".

This awakening could change your life forever.

Let us put those achievements under the microscope.

WE HAVE ALL THE ANSWERS!

A few years ago I went through a very traumatic phase in my relationship. It was time to decide whether or not to commit myself long-term. Having agonised over the decision for a few months, I decided to look for help. Having always believed that we have all the answers, I referred my dilemma to my powerful inner wisdom. Just before I went to sleep, I asked for help. I needed an answer. What should I do? My indecision was causing too much pain. The following weekend I spent a very pleasant time with my girlfriend. As I was driving away, seeds of doubt started to grow in my mind, maybe we shouldn't finish. Forget about it, I thought, lets listen to some music. The first song on the radio blasted out the message "time to say goodbye." Was this my answer, I wondered?

The next day I invested in some new tapes. As I was driving home a message came over loud and clear from the tape: "choice is the difference between selecting what you want and what you want more". Between what you want and what you want more. Again this statement resonated with me. I really, really liked this girl, more than anybody ever, but...

The straw that broke the camel's back was to happen the following day. I was visiting a new client. The conversation turned to relationships (unusual for a first meeting). A few years ago, he dated a girl who was, at the time, engaged. They got on superbly - "everything in every way was perfect," he told me. Each week they'd spend as much time as possible together! Suddenly the woman disappeared completely from the scene; the next time he heard from her she was married. Two years later, the newly-weds had separated. My colleague started meeting up with the woman again and at the opportune moment asked the all important question "why did you marry him when it was obvious you didn't love him?" She said "oh, all the wedding preparations had been completed; I felt sorry for him, I didn't want him to suffer."

I got a particular ill feeling that shot through my system like a tidal wave. Every time I was asked why I would not finish the relationship with my girlfriend, I responded "I don't want her to suffer." The universe had given me a very consistent answer. It was time to say goodbye. I accepted the verdict. Two weeks later, I parted company from my girlfriend.

I got a phone call from a colleague, Graeme, who was suffering with a slipped disk. He had been informed by his doctor that he was run down, and that the healing process was going to take a long time. Graeme is a business consultant with one of the largest consultancy firms in the world. Most of his life is spent going from country to country; assignment to assignment, finding little time to himself to 'be'...to relax. Graeme started to ponder over life's options, and decided after a 'chance' meeting with another colleague that maybe a sabbatical, some time off, was the order of the day. Sitting on his hotel room bed, he turned on the television. On the box was a programme about health. Interesting? OK, time for the news. After the news he switched channels. Again, new channel, programme topic: health. I get the message, he sighed. He has now set a goal to rebalance his life. Health now comes before wealth!

Reflections

You have all the answers, all that is necessary is 1. to ask; 2. to be aware.

Ask: The best time to ask is when you are relaxed, just before you go to sleep at night (the last ten to fifteen minutes are usually the most effective), before you leave your bed in the morning or during relaxation exercises which will be described in detail in future chapters.

Be 'Aware': Watch out for those apparent coincidences/ intuitions, those 'chance meetings', that inner wisdom. We get messages all the time...from the radio, from idle conversation and from chance meetings. Simply tune in for your answers. Some people tune out all their lives, they do not want to listen, then they cannot understand why their lives are less than fulfilled.

Have you experienced anything like this before?...Have you found answers...are you willing to listen?

C L E V E R   C H I L D !

Nothing is going to stop me!

By the age of five most people have learned how to walk. Learning how to walk was a very interesting process - you crawled, you got up on your feet, bang, fell face down, tried again, readapted, up again...bang, down again and so on...ultimately learning how to master the art. Furthermore, by five years of age you boasted a vocabulary of over 80% of the words necessary to communicate daily. Not impressed? Let's put those achievements in context. Would you get up and try again, with your current thought patterns, if you failed in your quest for a job once, twice, 10 times, 20 times, 30 times? With a similar thought process to a child, you would. What about attempting to become proficient in a new language, without the aid of any direct instruction, textbooks, tutorials...quite a challenge! Not so for the 'uninhibited child'. Free from the chains of social conditioning everything is possible.

It comes and goes!

Did you ever notice how a child can be crying one moment and in bliss moments later? How come we can't do this? It's because the clever child doesn't play the sad story over and over again in their mind. They let it go...They know how to master their emotional state.

The message is simple: **learn to act like a child**.

"If your mind is empty, it is always ready for anything; it is open to everything. In the beginner's mind there are many possibilities, in the expert's mind there are few" - Zen master Suzuki-Roshi.

THAT MAGNETIC POWER

If I was to ask you what are the biggest material decisions you have made or are likely to make in your life, it is highly probable that moving house or buying a car would feature prominently.

Because of their relative importance, a significant amount of time and energy is invested in these processes. When you think about anything at length it becomes ingrained in your subconscious mind. When that occurs, interesting things start to happen.

A few years ago, I decided to buy a new car. As my job involves quite a lot of driving, I am familiar with most Irish towns. This time the journey appeared different. Car dealerships seemed to appear! Amusingly, I couldn't recall seeing them in those spots before. Indeed in my local town it almost seemed as if the car dealer premises had a more imposing structure, had moved even closer to the road! Time for a rest, let's look at the paper... absolutely nothing in it except car adverts; as for the TV and radio, the only advertising revenue they were getting must have been from the motor industry! Finally I bought the car. I hoped I made the right choice...of course I did...over the next few days I saw many people driving the exact same car as mine!

What about you ? Think about a major purchase in your life, for example, your car. See if you can identify any parallels with my story. You will soon start to see that this magnetic power has been operating your whole life...your challenge is to start exploiting this resource - Now!!

Attracting teachers, they are waiting!

Have you ever noticed that teachers always seem to appear when you are ready to learn?

I recall pitching for a consultancy contract in the agriculture industry. The veterinary staff questioned my knowledge of the agriculture business. As I was raised in a shop and my interaction with the farming world was minimal, my existing knowledge was poor. I declared "nothing; but I'm a quick learner". Two weeks later, the contract was mine. Immediately I set about learning as much as possible about agriculture in as little time as possible. That night, after a presentation in a Monaghan town, I retired to a hotel lounge to watch a soccer match. I started to talk to the person beside me. It turned out that he was an agricultural consultant. I riddled him with a record-breaking number of 'dumb' questions! The following morning, before I got involved in the usual morning rituals, the names of potential teachers popped up in my mind...many of my friends were agricultural science graduates, others were big farmers. Two months later, the company vet could not understand how I had got a grasp of things so quickly (I, the student was ready!).

Reflection

When you dwell upon anything, it goes from your conscious mind to your subconscious. The more you think about it, the stronger the connections in your nervous system, the more deeply ingrained it becomes. Your subconscious has an efficient filtering system that on instruction will help you see what you want to see. More amazingly, it will attract into your life circumstances, people and information that will help you achieve your goal. To make the most out of these circumstances, you must be willing to adopt the most persuasive strategy in life: **ask 'dumb' questions** (more about that later).

When you truly commit yourself to a goal, any goal, and you passionately believe in a positive outcome, things start to happen which will make it a reality in the external world.

Think about times in your life where this magnetic power has manifested itself.

POSITIVE EXPECTATIONS WORKED!

"Optimism is the fault that leads to achievement" - Helen Keller

EVERY TIME I THINK SOMETHING POSITIVE IS GOING TO HAPPEN, IT DOES.

Disagree?

What about the number of people who go to their local GP with 'flu, a cold or whatever, and, without medication feel better after consultation. They expected to be cured, and were. What about those people who are cured after taking a placebo? The Placebo is something that has all the cosmetic qualities of a drug, but has no medicinal properties whatsoever. A study proving its effectiveness was conducted by Dr Beecher in Harvard University. Two groups were used in the experiment, one was administered morphine, the other a placebo. Both groups of post-operative patients were told they were being given something to relieve the pain. The pain was controlled in 52% of patients who received morphine, and in 40% of cases receiving the placebo. The conclusion: in many cases, people can cure themselves by just expecting a positive outcome; by just believing something works.

Belief is the most powerful drug in the world.

Seven years ago, I received a phonecall about my first potential contract. I had been advised that two local companies needed marketing training. To secure the contract, the procedure involved visiting each of the two companies. If they 'bought' me, the training was all mine; if they didn't like me, no job. I remember getting off the phone and rushing into my assistant Amanda exclaiming "we've got work!" On cross-examination, it was mentioned that I hadn't even met the client yet..."no problem," I declared," I'll get it...and I did. Before every sales presentation I see myself getting the deal. I become absolutely convinced there is no other eventuality and in the majority of cases there rarely is.

Remember when you believe the deal is inevitable you adopt that physiology. You walk, you talk with confidence and energy. Half the battle!

What about those people who don't need alarm clocks, confident they will wake up on time, regardless of what time that may be. Or indeed, those who expect to get a car parking space, mentally booking it in advance - even in the city!

Yes, positive expectations work, but the reverse is also true. *Negative expectations unfortunately work!*

EVERYTIME I THINK SOMETHING NEGATIVE IS GOING TO HAPPEN, IT DOES.

Popular self fulfilling prophecies:

☀ *"It is time to die."*

What about those who retire to die and do! Did you ever notice how dramatically some people age between 65 and 66, in contrast to the more gradual process 0 to 65?

Most people are programmed to believe that on reaching this one date in the calendar year 'their day is nigh'; they reach this age with no aspirations, no purpose, no longing and invariably wither and die.

Sometimes this 'death-wish' surfaces even earlier in life after the intervention of Dr Destiny! Let me explain.

As we all know, doctors are very much a revered species in the community, many people believe unconditionally what they have to say...why? - because the general consensus is *they know*. Thus, when Dr Destiny says "you have 6 months to live," some people accept this reality, prepare to die, and do, bang on time! It is my opinion that *nobody* knows, so for someone to give another person a deadline is not acceptable.

Indeed, children can also have a negative influence on the ageing process.

A group of older people was recently put through a training course conducted by my colleague, Mr Pat Campbell of FAS (Ireland's national training organisation). I was informed that the biggest challenge the participants encountered in life was the constant disempowering advice from their children. The problem was, they were not acting in accordance with their childrens' expectations: "You should not be doing that...You are not able to do that...Take it easy."

The reality is that, contrary to the prevailing wisdom, these people were never needed more.

1. The working world needs your experience.

With the current demographics in the industrial world, the ongoing involvement of the over 60s in the labour force is assured due to an acute shortage of skilled personnel. The 65+ age group is fast becoming the new age career people. Indeed, it is ironic that many of the more famous people's best work happened after the age of 65, Carl Jung, Verdi, among others.

As Martin Luther King advised: *"No one should retire from life at any age"*

2. The next generation needs you.

No one needs love more than the child setting out on his journey through life. There is nothing more potent, more valuable, than the unconditional love shown to children by grandparents. In the prevailing 'nanny culture', where children are allowed limited access to their parents, I cannot overemphasise the importance of this role.

Regardless, you deserve to relax; to be; to pursue your interests and hobbies.

The bottom line - prepare for your retirement as you prepared for other significant events in your life...expect to enjoy it; watch what happens.

☀ *"It is going to be a dreadful day!"*
We all know the story about people who wake up in the morning and keep saying to themselves "oh, today is going to be awful"...and it is. Those horrible self fulfilling prophecies...

☀ *"Don't hit the water!"*
What about those golf enthusiasts who, before they swing their golf clubs, have an internal voice, which, like a tape, is playing over and over again "don't hit it in the water"...and it finds water!

☀ *"I am going to get sick!"*

Even more wondrous, how about those people who successfully invite diseases which duly arrive. "Oh! There's a 'flu bug going around...I always catch it." How come I can never catch these bugs! Indeed, for years I have battled with my father over the necessity for health insurance. My opinion: what's the point - I'm not into disease. Is there method in my madness?

☀ *"I will not play well!"*

My soccer career! We were playing the county final. I had played quite well by my standards on the run-up to the match, having scored a few goals. That day, one of the lads was late; for whatever reason I started to believe I was going to have a disastrous match. I wasn't wrong! I was substituted for the first time in my life in the first half. All my team-mates agree, if they are running in on goal, and a negative thought crosses their mind like "you are gonna miss, gonna miss," they usually do.

So what's the message?

Our lives are not moulded so much by our experience but our expectations...expect the best!

Y O U   A R E   I N T E L L I G E N T !

I'm not intelligent enough!

Well, which intelligence are you referring to...do you believe that linguistic intelligence, i.e. being verbally elite; having the alphabet after your name, is a true monitor? This is a flawed analysis, considering the number of 'intelligent people' that do not get past the first job interview because of their inability to communicate; their inability to prosper in the university of life. What about your interpersonal intelligence, i.e. the ability to get on well with people, the ability to understand, empathise with other people, know how they are feeling? How do you rate? That is a very important skill. What about your intrapersonal intelligence, the ability to know oneself, to motivate oneself, to take action.

Interesting...interpersonal and intrapersonal are the most highly paid intelligences in the world. Both are accessible to most, and you don't need a PhD to qualify! Maybe you are destined to become the next great architect or interior designer using your high degree of spatial intelligence, or indeed, with your musical intelligence...the next Mozart. What about being the next sporting hero (bodily/kinesthetic intelligence)?

What's my point? It is time we moved away from our flawed analysis which argues that grades imply intelligence. Everybody possesses all of Harvard University's Howard Gardner's '7 intelligences' in varying degrees. Indeed, as all of them can positively contribute to your growth and happiness...you are intelligent!

W H A T   A   P H A R M A C Y !

Each day the human body creates billions of cells. Our skin changes once a month, liver every 6 weeks, stomach lining every 5 days, even our skeleton changes every 3 months.

During deep relaxation the body produces calming chemicals in the right amounts which it sends to the right area and with no side effects! Interesting, when one considers the following fact: Last year in America approximately $1bn was spent on pills to help people overcome the side-effects of other drugs.

During times when you feel absolutely exhilarated, like when you are riding a rollercoaster, your body produces the cancer treatment drug interferon/interlucon in the right amounts delivered to the right area with no side effects. A similar course from the pharmacy would cost you thousands of pounds.

While you read this book the power within is regulating your breathing, controlling your blood supply, recreating your body.

...And you believe you aren't powerful!

YOU CAN RECREATE
EXCELLENCE ON REQUEST!

Did you ever notice how listening to one of your favourite songs can immediately raise your spirits, while another song can evoke sad memories, immediately damping your spirits? Or how, on seeing the national flag being raised, you immediately experience an adrenaline rush through your system. What we are describing here is how one event in time, something you see, hear, taste, whatever, can change the way you feel instantaneously.

Just imagine if you could make yourself feel empowered on request...The good news is you can!

Music does it for me!
Did you ever hear a song which changed the way you felt instantaneously from happy to sad, from down to exhilarated?

Everytime I hear *"Be not afraid...I stand before you"* I become sad. When I first heard the song at Knock, the Pope was anointing people one of whom came from my home town. The whole experience really touched me. I began to associate the song with these feelings. Now, any time I hear this song, I immediately find myself in bad humour. For many, when they hear *"Candle In The Wind"* by Elton John, they will immediately relive the emotion they experienced on the day Princess Diana was laid to rest.

Alternatively, I hear other songs like *"Simply the Best"* and I feel empowered, because of an experience associated with the song. For many people, the national anthem is an empowering trigger.

In summary, the music is the anchor.

Just a taste!
Playing the lead in the school production of "My Fair Lady" in front of a sell-out crowd was always going to be a thrilling experience for Orla. As part of the build-up she was under teacher's instructions to keep her voice in shape. To achieve the desired result, every day she got a packet of Vicks from her mentor to keep her voice moist. The show was a huge success. Three

months later, while out shopping, one of her colleagues who had a cold offered her a Vicks. Amazingly, the minute the lozenge connected with her taste buds, feelings of exhilaration and nervous excitement were triggered off in her body. She was reliving her musical experience. The taste was the anchor!

Just a Touch!
Think about when someone special in your life died. At the funeral people are offering their condolences. Many patting you on the shoulder in sympathy, others shaking hands. It is not unusual for people to relive these emotions months later when someone comes up and taps them on the shoulder. Some can reignite this emotion just by shaking hands. The touch is the anchor.

Just a quick flash!
Some people can immediately change state on seeing, for example, their national flag being raised.

What has happened?
When you are in a peak emotional state, any trigger, anything you see around you, anything you hear in the background, a person's touch, even a taste becomes associated with the experience. When you see that object or hear that sound, the event and associated feelings immediately come flooding back into your system. Very simply, you could be feeling down one moment, anchor triggered, you feel great!

Anchoring is an incredibly powerful technique. Before any major presentation, I take time out, retreat to a place where I won't be disturbed, close my eyes and remember the last presentation I completed which went excellently. I run through the whole experience in my mind, reliving the feeling, simultaneously saying to myself - "this will be excellent, this will be excellent, I am ready for action, feeling fine."

Anchoring is very powerful, it always happens when you are in a peak emotional state, positive or negative.

How do you anchor yourself.? Let us look at a few ways.
How can we recreate excellence on request?

ACTION 1

Power Music!

Note: When we close our eyes and relax, the majority of us see images flashing in front of us. It is as if we are sitting in a cinema, only this time the screen is within ourselves. This is what I mean when I talk about the mental screen.

Objective: Create a positive anchor which will allow you to feel empowered on request.

For those who like music, choose the following plan of action.

Retreat to your favourite place, remember a time in your life when you felt really strong, everything was just fantastic. See what you saw, hear what you heard, feel how you felt. Feeling great, turn on the music. Now, as you relive this experience in your mind, brighten it up, bring it closer in your mind's eye, make it the size of your mental screen, make it a full colour, surround-sound movie, relive these experiences in full...enjoy yourself.

Do this once or twice every day for five days.

Your mind should have started to associate the music with this intense positive feeling. Try it out. Turn on the music. How do you feel? If you get that special feeling again, you've got it, otherwise keep working on the association. When you *have* got it, the trick is to play the music before any significant event in your life, when you need to feel empowered. Imagine walking into that important interview, shoulders back, feeling empowered, totally relaxed.

Just one touch/Just one word!

Again, retreat to your favourite place, think of a time when you felt really, really fantastic. Relive the experience in full, see what you were seeing, hear what you were hearing, relive the feeling. As you think about it brighten up the movie more, make it full colour, bring it closer in your minds eye, make the event the size of your mental screen, add in sound, relive those feelings. When you are getting that special feeling, say a word unique to you or use a kinesthetic trigger, e.g. press your index finger at the nail, hold it while you are really enjoying the experience. Hold throughout the experience, then get up and move around.
Come back, run through the experience again. Remember when you are feeling great to press your index finger nail, holding it throughout the experience. Run this experiment 5/6 times, now let's test it.
As you squeeze the nail on your index finger, how do you feel. Are you getting that special feeling back? What happens when you repeat the word?

Keep working at it until the association is in place.

"One must always remember that every man in a sense represents the whole of humanity and its history. What was possible in the history of mankind at large is also possible on a small scale in every individual. What mankind has needed may eventually be needed by the individual too" - Carl Jung.

Conclusion

For years I have listened to the uninspired attribute people's happiness to luck, to coincidences, to external events. After your awakening, you can understand why I always dismissed those notions. In my opinion the critic was just looking for excuses to justify his current situation. The reality is amazing. Things start to happen when we commit ourselves to adding value to the universe, when we expect a positive outcome. If you make the decision to act now you will find that teachers will appear, circumstances will conspire to show you the way. In summary, you will notice you have all the resources you need, regardless of your background/current situation.

ACTION 3

Time to wake up!

Objective: To become more aware

Get a notepad/pencil. Note all the 'apparent coincidences/ intuitions;' those 'inner knowings' in your life. Follow this on by noting your dreams.
Is the universe giving you a message?

※

"I wake up from dreams and go: 'Wow! Put this down on paper'. You hear the words, everything is there in front of your face. That's why I hate to take credit for songs I've written. I feel that somewhere, someplace it has been done and I'm just a courier bringing it into the world" - Michael Jackson.

ACTION 4

Expect the best!

Objective: Begin with the end in mind, put the desired outcome in movie form in your mind.

Let's assume you are planning for that job interview. It does not matter what the event is, as long as it is something you **really want** in your life.

Procedure - close your eyes, relax, focus in on your breathing, follow the rise and fall of your abdomen as you breathe in and out. Imagine that you are inhaling clear blue air and exhaling grey toxic air. Visualise what you are wearing; the people on the interview board; the room; the plants; the view through the window. Notice how confident you look. See the interviewers nod their heads in agreement as you speak.

Now associate with this image, move into this body as if you were there seeing through your eyes, feeling very confident, delighted with the positive feedback you are getting from the panel. Notice how confident your projection is.

Note that fantastic feeling you are getting as you handle all the questions with ease and confidence. Listen to yourself answering with assurance. Notice the feelings generated when the owner comments how delighted he is that you could make the interview and looks forward to speaking to you in greater detail in the future. Intensify that feeling, feel the warmth of the people's handshake on departure. Truly this has been an excellent experience.

Return to this movie, every night just before you go to sleep or in relaxation periods, when your brain is running at alpha levels of consciousness (this is a state of relaxed alertness allowing you to imprint your desired reality on your subconscious).

Create the desired movie in the mind...watch what happens.

Mental rehearsal, i.e. running the desired outcome in movie format, is not a new phenomenon. Did you ever watch athletes lining up for a track event? Notice how focused they look, almost as if they are in a trance. What is happening? They are running the race in their mind. In fact, it is likely they will have run the race in their mind 20 or 30 times before they start. It is critical we begin with the end in mind - the *fait accompli*. This is powered by the fuel - *belief*. What about those footballers or rugby players who have a certain routine when they are taking frees or penalty kicks. What is happening? You can bet that ball has gone over the bar hundreds of times in their minds...it pays to rehearse!

Remember your external world is a mirror reflection of your internal world.

ACTION ▅ 5

Empowering words.

Objective: Appreciating the power of words on our nervous system, filter everything at source.

For example, next time you are about to say "problem," change to "challenge"; change "failure" to "learning experience;" "it can't be done" to "we are going to find a way." Nothing is impossible. Change "there is nothing I can do" to "if it is to be, it is up to me"...and so on.

Change your vocabulary to include only positive, constructive, responsible language.

"Spoken words are the symbol of mental experience" - Aristotle.

What have you learned?

How are you going to benefit from this new knowledge?

2

GOING SOMEWHERE OR GOING NOWHERE

"Without a vision a man shall perish" - Proverb.

Just imagine going into your favourite department store, looking around never asking for anything, or worse still not knowing what you want. What are the likely outcomes? I suppose if you stay there long enough you'll probably be thrown out! Or maybe you will end up with something you don't want.

Let us now assume this department store is life, what have you got to do? Know what you want and be willing to ask for it. This chapter deals with this critical issue - the art of goalsetting, exploring in detail - the art of knowing **what** to ask followed by the art of knowing **how** to ask.

Finally at the end of this chapter the merits of goalsetting are discussed.

I DON'T KNOW WHAT TO ASK FOR?

No matter what audience I address, parents, teachers, students or business owners, sooner or later someone, in a cry for help will declare:

"but I don't know what I should do!"

In my experience this is the biggest challenge most people encounter. Most of us go through life not knowing what we want, but feeling pretty sure our current reality isn't it! Ironically enough, you *do* know, everybody has a purpose. Everybody has some unique talent that, if exploited, would make the passage a more fulfilling journey. Usually it is so obvious we oftentimes dismiss it - *"that can't be it!"* By becoming more aware you will uncover your mission. You will pinpoint your unique talent.

Let us unearth this mission!

ACTION 🎬 6

Mission identification...Mission Possible!

Objective: By highlighting your values and interests you can unearth your mission. Values are judgements we make about what is important, in our lives, what makes life worth living.

A mission is a sense of purpose that propels you into the future. Living your mission will truly reignite the fire within.

Pen and paper required, please.

☀ Write down what you really love doing in life; things that you are passionately interested in. For example, a subject you love talking to people about, reading books about, watching TV programmes about, listening to on the radio - an area in which the person you most admire works...Indeed, you love it so much you don't need to get paid to do it because the feelings it generates are on their own worth the investment. Note the feeling generated by indulging in these 'interesting' activities.

☀ What do you currently value most in life? What feelings are generated by satisfying these values?

Tip: Note past extreme reactions to experiences, what made you angry, what values had been violated? What about feeling fulfilled, exhilarated? What values were being satisfied? In these emotional peaks you will find a person's values. Note underlying values underpinning your goals.

Write down the first things that come into your mind without exhaustive analysis. List them, starting with the most important.

I recall discussing this exercise with one of my review group, who declared "I just can't do this." OK. I advised her to respond to the following question, "what would you do if you knew you had only one month to live?". "Travel the world?" "So, you value fun and adventure?" "Oh, yes." There's an answer. Continuing, her eyes moist with excitement, she declared how she would absolutely love to lecture on communication, after she was married and had a family...And she didn't know what she wanted!

Examples of values: Humour; love; excellence; challenge; mastery; wisdom; contribution; fun; honesty; freedom; security; perseverance.

What is your mission? Remember goals in conflict with your mission are like having a Ferrari with no fuel.

☼ What occupation/field of experience could give you the feelings generated by your top values and interests? What job fits in with your mission? Will this job allow you to do what you love and love what you do? Be imaginative. Discuss what you have written with someone you trust.

Reflection
We don't do things for things' sake! We do them for the feelings generated internally as a result. We don't value cars, houses, money, holidays: what we really value is the feelings generated from these things, for example love, freedom, independence, security, passion, comfort.

The advertising agencies have been aware of this for years. They don't sell products, they sell feelings.

Furthermore if your goals fit in with your values and your interests, the foundation for success is in place. It is unlikely you will have problems motivating yourself to do something you love.

Can you recall a time in your life when you were sitting lethargically at home, looking forward to nothing but a good sleep, and your friend dashes in the door, "interested in going to (a movie; a match; a concert)?" Suddenly you experience a mad flush of energy sweeping through your body. The lethargic state had lifted miraculously. If pursuing your goal is accompanied by the same energy, you have truly discovered your mission.

VIG = Very important guidelines for goalsetting, don't forget it.
G = R(V + I)
Goals should be a reflection of your values and interests.

One of my primary goals in life was to be in a position to impart my ideology to all types of people from all around the world. My core value was to make a difference, to positively add value to peoples lives - my primary occupation, motivational speaker...totally in tune with my interests and values. No wonder I enjoy it so much. It is not a job, it is a hobby (standing up in front of hundreds of people, a holiday? - for me, yes!)

ACTION 7

Time to Ask!

Objective: To tune into your higher power, which will give you the necessary instructions/directions.

Ask!

Just before you go to sleep at night or before you fully awake in the morning or during relaxation exercises, ask for help! Imagine you are inhaling fresh blue air, circulating this air around your heart and exhaling all the toxins and waste. Continue focusing on your heart area until you feel relaxed, then simply repeat in your mind - *"my goal is to find my mission, please help me!"*

Be alert. Tune in. Get ready for that answer. It may not be immediate, and your answer could come later in the form of lessons from new teachers, intuitions or dreams. It is important you note all on paper. As you review what you have written, what is the message? Only **you** will know. *You do know.*

H O W   D O   I   A S K ?

Here is a test for those who know what they want. Let us speculate that you have won the Lotto: would this change your mission? Yes? I suggest you go back to mission identification stage! What do you see yourself doing in 10/20 years time, radically different to what you are currently doing? It is obvious that your current role is not aligned with your mission. Following your mission ensures that you end up doing something you love doing, something from which you generate much pleasure, something you will always want to do regardless of the circumstances.

In this section let us assume you know what you want. Next dilemma: how do you ask?

THE ISSUES

As you set out your vision for the future it is essential to honour the following guidelines:-

▷ Accept the importance of balance in your life.
▷ Make sure your goals will achieve what you really want.
▷ Recognise the power of clarity.
▷ Set a time limit.
▷ Break your vision down into manageable steps.
▷ Be realistic yet optimistic.
▷ Focus on your vision, the map will appear.
▷ Do not let anyone dampen your enthusiasm...unless they are very well informed!

▷ Know why you passionately want to achieve the vision.
▷ Set a plan for their achievement.
▷ Celebrate your experiences.
▷ Imprint goals on your subconscious.

Let us look at these issues in detail.

☀ Go for Balance

"One man cannot do right in one department of life whilst he is occupied in doing wrong in any other department, life is one indivisible whole" - Gandhi

Set goals for all the different parts of your life:-

▷ Relationships with family and partner.
▷ Spiritual.
▷ Personal Development.
▷ Business/Financial.
▷ Health/Lifestyle Goals.
▷ Community/Charity.

Never forget "all work and no play makes Jack a dull boy."
Balance must be the goal for those who suffer from addictions; those who over-value possessions (materialism); those who are addicted to (like myself until recently) work; to alcohol or drugs etc. If they are honest, they will notice their addictions have not delivered what they really want - happiness. Balance is the way towards a more fulfilling life.

The challenge is to work on the deprived areas of your life...adding a glass of water to a full bath does not make a major impact.

☀ It's got to be personal

It must be something that you really want from the heart, not your parents' goal, not your partner's goal, but **your** goal. Otherwise, it just won't happen. As an aside, too much pressure is put on children to conform to their parents' expectations rather than pursuing what they want in life.

☀ The power of clarity

Your brain works in the specific, so goals must be delivered in that style.
"I want to be happy" is not a goal. Why?
You cannot measure it. If I give you £5, you are happy for that moment. Does that mean you have achieved your goal? It's not specific enough. Ask yourself these questions: "How would you know if you were happy? Where would you be if you were really happy?" Maybe then your goal will change to: "I have a foreign holiday annually".

Examples of specific goals:-
▷ "I weigh 250 kg.
▷ "I help 5 people annually to achieve their goal.
▷ "I earn £25,000 a year."

I heard a great story about three women who decided to go for a day out to Dublin. Two of them were on a mission: to find a suitable man. The third, who was at the time in a religious order, had been roped in to do the chauffeuring. As they approached their chosen destination a request was placed with the driver for some divine intervention. She promised she would arrange it. After dropping them off, she went away and did her own thing. The following day, they met up. The partygoers appeared quite agitated. They had indeed met some gentlemen, who had cordially accompanied them to a dinner dance. Unfortunately, they arrived, ate the dinner and left. "Did you pray for us at all?" they questioned. "Yes, the woman commented, but you didn't tell me you wanted the men to stay with you as well!" The message - be specific: ask for what you want!

☀ Time Please!

You must have a specific time frame for the achievement of each goal.

Currently you weigh 336kg. The goal must be that you expect to weigh 250kg by no later than 24 months from now. Many people do not set deadlines for their goals, which is as good as opting out. Come back to those people in 1-2-5 years time, they are still going for it (in their minds!), but ultimately going nowhere.

Break down your goals from overall purposes in life to 10 year, 5 year, 1 year, monthly, weekly, daily goals. Don't be a gonna doer!

☀ Chunking

A guarantee: some people shy away from goalsetting because they do not believe they can achieve big goals. By breaking these goals into small steps (which in most cases can be immediately worked upon, either today or tomorrow), when they succeed, they start to believe that the world is their oyster. One of my course participants commented on the completion of a small step: "I felt brilliant. It was something I was putting off for a while. You know, now I think everything is possible." Why does this happen? For most people their problem is they cannot take action - that's the issue. When they conquer that challenge at any level everything becomes possible.

"A journey of a thousand miles starts with a single step" - *Lao Tzu.*

☀ Be realistic yet optimistic

Sounds confusing? Let me explain. Some people set goals that are unachievable by us mortals, e.g. "everybody will respond positively to all my presentations," "I'll be happy when I know everybody respects and loves me." The trend: perfection orientated goals that just are not realistic.

But, ironically, my biggest problem with people is that what they see as realism, I would interpret as pessimism. Here is a sample of goals I have set in the past:

1. With an empty pocket in 1994 I set a goal that within 2 years I would attend a course in Colorado, which required a major investment. Subgoal was to achieve *Neuro Linguistic Programming Practitioner status when I got there. That was the easy part.

2. The goal in 1995 was to speak at a minimum of two national conferences in 1996. Yes, this unknown Roscommon man was going to get invited to speak at National Conferences.

Both goals were achieved, more about the strategy later.

So what's the message? In two words, s t r e t c h y o u r s e l f . It is only when you wander outside your comfort zone you see just how incredibly powerful you are. The greatest temptation in life is to declare, *"OK, it'll do"* - settling for little or less. *"If I don't aim high, I won't be disappointed if I don't succeed"* is an opt out!

"No man can discover new oceans unless he has the courage to lose sight of the shores." - Anonymous.

My advice is simple - commit yourself to achieving your goal, focus completely on the goal, and the map will appear. You don't need to know everything right away, otherwise it wouldn't be a goal. As an aside, remember how you spoke your first language before you learned how to do it?

---

*NLP (Neuro Linguistic Programming) - which stands for Neuro, our nervous system, the mental pathways of our five senses by which we see, hear, feel, taste, and smell; Linguistic, refers to our ability to use language and how specific words and phrases, mirror our mental worlds. In addition, it refers to our silent language of postures, gestures and habits that reveal our thinking styles, beliefs and more; Programming is borrowed from computer science, to suggest that our thoughts, feelings and actions are simply habitual programs that can be changed by upgrading our mental software.

☀ Who should I tell?

This issue will be covered in more detail in chapter 7: "Choose who to listen to."

This is a critical challenge. Some people are afraid to disclose their goals, fearing derision or feedback that may hinder their progress.

Three quick suggestions.

1. Don't tell anybody!
The only person that needs to be convinced is you; your goals need only to be realistic to you, nobody else.

2. Let them go!
Obviously your 'friends,' your confidantes, have not got the wherewithal to take you to a new level. Time to create a group of new mentors, to show you the way, in that particular challenge.

3. Let it Go!
Derision and laughter from people who will resent your energy and enthusiasm are all part of the journey. You show your maturity by letting it go; not reacting.

☀ Do you really want to reach these goals?!

Reasons please! - write down why you want to reach these goals. Remember these reasons must fit with your interests and values in order to have real power. The more reasons you have, the more likely you are to be motivated to achieve them. Note: we don't want to reach goals like having a new house or a new car just for the sake of having more things. Instead, we want the feelings generated by having a new car or new home; those maybe of independence, of liberty etc.

"We don't do things for things sake, we do them for the feelings we get when we have achieved them "

Indeed, sometimes we end up after finishing our journey with the appropriate feelings but not the things we specified initially. Congratulations you have been successful!

☀ The Cunning Plan

How can you achieve these goals? What has to be done? Jot down all the necessary steps as you see it; what are your current abilities; what do you need to learn; who can help you; who are the best mentors? Remember, it is unlikely you have the exact map, otherwise they wouldn't be goals.

☀ Celebrate!

Celebrate your achievements, otherwise why should you bother climbing the next mountain? Celebration can take any form: a holiday abroad or a nice cup of tea. You deserve it!

ACTION 🎬 8

Motivational Movie Time

Objective: To create the motivational movie in your mind and to make it available on request.

Find a nice quiet place where you will not be disturbed. Relax, focus on your breathing: in - out, in - out, in - out. To relax even further, imagine you are sitting in a beautiful location, the birds singing around you, the sun splitting the stones. Everything is perfect. Now imagine that your dreams have come true. Something you have wanted all your life is now yours.

You can see yourself in that job, or having that relationship or whatever you desire. Now step into the movie so you imagine being there, doing what you really want to do. You see the people;

you hear them speaking positively to you; you feel the excitement of having achieved your goal; being involved in something you love.

As you run this movie in your mind I have a simple question for you: are you excited? If not, something is wrong. If yes, continually run this movie in your mind, appreciating Descartes' comments *"I think, therefore I am."*

The next time you run the movie, experiment with the following:
▷ If, as you see it in your mind, it is only a still picture, change it to a movie.
▷ If it is black and white; change it to colour.
▷ If it is a small image located on your mental screen; change it, making it the size of the screen.
▷ If it is a dull colour; make it brighter.
▷ If it is far away in your minds eye, bring it closer.
▷ Add in your favourite motivational song to the movie.

Do any of these changes make a difference to the way you feel about the goal? Whichever movie energises you, persist with it. Never forget your external world is a mirror reflection of your internal world.

☀ Administering goals - the nitty gritty
Aim: All tasks are designed with one aim in mind - to imprint the desired reality in your subconscious. In other words, to make the universe aware of your desires.

Write down your goals!
Imperative: when they are in your head, they are up in the air; non-committal.

Write in the following style, 1. personal: i.e. "I"; 2. positive: e.g. "I visit two countries annually."

Ensure that you ask for what you want, not what what you don't want. Why? Unfortunately, when you say "I don't want to be fat," your brain cannot understand negatives and flips up the most relevant image on your mental screen (yes "one of you being fat") and subsequently works on it.

Maybe that's why my "I don't want to smoke", "I don't want to be fat" goals never work! For a better outcome, say: "I weigh 250kg!"

Finally, speak in the present tense. Visualise it as a completed task; let your inner wisdom show you the way. "I am an international motivational speaker."

When your goals are personal, positive and stated as if they have been achieved, they are more convincing to your subconscious mind.

Rewrite on an ongoing basis. Remember, everytime you rewrite your goals you are imprinting them on your subconscious.

By using all three mediums, it sees your words, it hears your voice (when you write, you talk to yourself) and feels the movement along the page...

It is a good idea to write goals on index cards, putting them in your wallet or pocket. Have them where you can refer to them at all times. A goals review in the morning is recommended.

Unified effort!
When declaring your goals to the universe, ensure that your physiology is in tune. This is the one reason why most affirmation programmes do not work. Affirmations are when you say something to yourself over and over again in the hope of imprinting it on your subconscious. For the programme to work, it needs one necessary improvement... passion/energy. "I earn £25,000 per annum" delivered in a bubbly, energetic voice projection is much more effective than delivered in a neutral one. In addition, regurgitating affirmations when you are sitting like a couch potato, shoulders slumped, head down, is not very convincing. Your subconscious will believe your body language more than the words you speak. Don't expect a positive outcome! To be successful, your voice, your body language, your words must all project the desired reality.

Draw your goal.

Place the drawing on your wall where you can review it on an ongoing basis. Don't worry, it doesn't have to be a Van Gogh! Why?

The more exposure you get to an illustration of what you want in life, the more it sinks deeper into your subconscious.

Tip: Make the drawing big!

Goal Setting - My Strategy

For each goal I select, before I go to sleep at night I create the movie in my mind. (e.g. I saw myself at the Neuro-Linguistic Programming training centre in Colorado, interacting with other participants, listening to their comments, feeling the buzz at being at the best training centre in the world.) This movie was backed up with the fuel that makes things happen - a firm belief in a positive outcome. The same strategy was used for the conference goal.

GOALS - DO THEY WORK?

In life - yes!

Before I invested time and energy in goalsetting, I read an interesting study which had been completed in the USA. In this they tracked the fortunes of Harvard University graduates. It was discovered that, after 10 years, the 3% who had set written goals, with specific plans for their achievement were worth more in economic terms than the other 97% combined. In addition, the divorce rate was lower in the 3% than in the 97%.

In life, looking forward to something in addition to living for the moment are necessary ingredients. Our initial discussion in Chapter 1 on the "third age employees" (those aged 65 and over) shows how important it is to have a purpose in life. Keep active: keep planning: it's the best medicine.

In the recruitment process, yes!

Let me explain - when I am interviewing people, it is inevitable that I will ask the candidate: "Is this job for you?" or a variation on the theme. In most cases, the answers come in the form of undiluted waffle: "Well, yes. I think I would be very good at the job. I think I'd relish the opportunity... (all generalities, no specifics)". Then the focussed applicant arrives on the scene. Responding to the question immediately, they will answer in the following fashion: "Well, yes. Three years ago, I decided that I wanted to be a nurse. The following summer I worked in a nursing home where I observed at first hand what nursing involved. I got a great sense of personal satisfaction watching people under my care, becoming healthier and happier. While there, I spoke at length to the staff nurses about their role. This gave me an in-depth insight into the challenges facing them on a daily basis..."

Without going on, it was obvious that this person wanted the job; it was part of her dream. What is more, she had taken action in the context of its achievement. In contrast, our earlier participant didn't know what he wanted. Indeed, more than likely any job would do. Any professional recruitment agent detecting this will eliminate this person immediately.

Bottom line: if you don't know what *you* want...you will find it difficult to get anything.

The final proof!

No matter who you speak to, they invariably have a problem with the following reality:

"Imagination is more important than knowledge" - *Albert Einstein.*

The question is, how can you put something in your mind that is not real and expect it to happen! You can, this is what I have been doing for years.

OK. Let's have some fun - a simple demonstration:

ACTION 🎬 9

Time to make a stand!

Objective: A demonstration of how your subconscious will work to make your external world a mirror reflection of your internal world.

Stand up! Come on now (nobody's looking, you're all right). Put your feet together and extend your left arm straight out directly in front of you until it is parallel to the ground or higher. Keeping your eyes focused directly in front of you, rotate your arm around until you can't go any further without moving your feet from the ground. Notice how far you got, by focusing on anything on the wall; something distinguishable that will help you.

Now, go back to your original position, arms down by your side, standing straight up. Close your eyes and, without moving, imagine on your mental screen doing the exact same exercise, but this time as you do it you go further; see yourself going further; feel the excitement of having conquered this challenge. (If you find that you can't visualise - 95%+ of people can - all that is required is for you to relax, just relax. Focus on your breathing, in...out, in...out, in...out. Now try again). When you are happy, i.e. when you can see yourself doing it in your mind, open your eyes, and complete the excercise again. Notice anything? Did you go further?. Yes...? Excellent! Out of the thousands I have brought through this exercise, 80%+ succeeded.

So what has this exercise shown us? By using our imagination we went further! **Why?** Success begins in the mind. Input your desired reality and enjoy what happens. Furthermore, your subconscious cannot differentiate between real and imagined events; whatever is inputted with belief is accepted and then worked upon with the aim of manifesting this in the real world. 💥

The final challenge

Take one step in the achievement of any of your goals before you complete the book.

"Making a beginning is one third of the work" - Irish Proverb

Time for the worst kept secret in the world:

My goal is to make this book a best-seller in Ireland within 9 months of its launch. To achieve my goal I must reach out to over 15,000 people with my message in the given time frame. As this hasn't happened before in this country, the sceptics are out in full force. "It won't happen"..."It can't happen"...Interesting...Remember, the past is not the future!

ACTION ■ 10

Objective: Most people are either motivated by the feelings generated when they are successful (moving towards pleasure) or motivated by a major urge to avoid pain at all cost. The first exercise (a) works with those motivated by pleasure, the second (b) with those who don't want pain! You will find one will motivate more than the other. For one of my colleagues on the review panel, the second exercise worked better: "no pain at all costs!" that is her motto. Whatever works...do it!.

A. Do it for pleasure.
Describe the type of person you want to be in five years time. Choose what ever time period you desire; personality type; where will you live; how you will spend your time. Let's have the full story. Just imagine you are this person, living in your dream house, enjoying excellent relationships with your partner and your family, travelling to your chosen destination. How does it feel?
(Can be for 5/10/20 years. The choice, as in everything, is all yours.)
If this vision doesn't excite you, move on...

B. Do it to avoid pain.
Imagine it is now the year 2003. All your life you have decided that talking was a more efficient way of living than taking action.
You've ended up in an unfulfilling relationship; in an "OK, it'll do" job; living in a less than desirable house; continuing to muse over what could have been; unable to give your children the kind of love they need, and, in short, are unhappy.

How do you feel? Is this what you want?

If not, it is time to take some positive action...the only choice.

"If you reach for the moon and miss, do not fret, for you are amongst the stars" - W.B. Yeats

Conclusion

Go for goals in every aspect of your life; from relationships (attracting the desired partner into your life); to business (getting that job); to sporting (achieving physical fitness); to community (dedicating time and energy monthly to building a better community). Why? Because, as we discovered in Chapter 1, you have all the resources you need. All that is required is for you to ask, and **you shall receive**. You now know how to ask! Come on, let's start the journey now! Under the headings outlined in this chapter, write down goals under each category. Write them down as quickly as you can - don't think about them. Now edit your list until you come up with your most important goals. Be specific! What's the time frame? What's the plan? Go for it!

Setting goals, and even more importantly working on them, is the most empowering, life transforming activity you will carry out. You will feel the buzz that comes with taking control of your life. Take this seriously. Trust with your heart and watch your life become one of adventure and magic.

Reflection

What have you learned?

How are you going to benefit from this new knowledge?

3

CARPE DIEM...
SIEZE
THE DAY

In this chapter the spotlight shines on the key competency in life:

communication.

The goal of effective communication must be to elicit the 'do I know you from somewhere' response on a first encounter. This is the ability to build instant rapport: to make people feel relaxed, to be able to connect under any circumstances. It opens the door to more successful relationships at home, in the community and at work.

Many 'gurus' have argued that to become an affective communicator one should speak in the other persons language. This is an oversimplistic view. Remember the last time you met someone for the first time and how you just didn't like them, regardless of how well they spoke? Yes, your use of language plays a part, but not the leading role. To get the chemistry right you should 'walk in their shoes.' To successfully walk in their shoes we have got to be able to make some assumptions about human nature, and we can. The bottom line is: we unique human beings are very predictable.

In the first part of the chapter, we show just how predictable we are; in the second half, techniques to build better relationships are discussed.

10 BILLION BRAIN CELLS YET SO PREDICTABLE?

☼ People Cannot Lie.

You cannot see in people's minds, but you can see their physiology! If you are 'aware,' no one will deceive you. Their words may say 'yes' but it will be crystal clear from the change in body language or voice projection (for example usually eye contact goes astray or a change in posture is recorded) that what they really meant to say was no. Words just got in the way!

When you appreciate that your *psychology* affects your *physiology* and vice-versa, you will never be fooled again. As an interviewer, I find it hard to believe that someone who walks in, shoulders slumped, flushed face, gives you a weak handshake, offers limited eye contact, speaks in a shaky voice projection and continues to behave in this way throughout the interview, is confident and possesses good interpersonal skills.

I exaggerate, but the truth is when you become aware, no one can fool you. Remember when you meet someone for the first time, 55% of your decision on whether you like them or not is based on their body language; 38% on their voice projection; 7% on their words.

We pay more attention to posture, head movements, the way people walk and their voice projection (remember your voice is the first indicator of stress) than we do to words. Communication, it is more than words.

An example from the recruitment world:
The most common mistake made at interviews: the jobseeker focuses his/her attention on the welcoming face on the interview panel while avoiding eye contact with the unfriendly one. Lack of eye contact implies lack of confidence, and in most interview situations guarantees rejection, no matter how colourful their vocabulary is.

❋ PEOPLE LOVE TO BE HEARD
You are assured that the following strategy will endear you to people:-

Active Listening.
Listen with your eyes and ears. Why? People love to hear the sound of their own voices. Some go into a trance when they are speaking; they are in ecstasy when you give them your undivided attention (you are subtly sending them this critical message: "what you have to say is important," thus feeding their ego).

An extension of this strategy is to listen to what they say and repeat it back to them later on in the conversation. "You mentioned earlier the importance of ...". I attended the Garth Brooks concert in 1997. He is not only a great musician, but a very tuned-in marketing person. Garth declared that the thing that really hits artists right there (gesturing at his heart) is when the crowd sing their songs back to them. Well of course it does Garth!

Furthermore, remember that when you let people talk, sooner or later they will tell you what to say, as long as you are aware!

"Talk to people about themselves and they'll listen for hours" - Benjamin Disraeli

It is no coincidence that God gave us two ears, two eyes and one mouth.

So why don't we use those eyes and ears? Unfortunately, too many of us are not good listeners. This is not clever. We have all met an irritating sales person who never shuts up, or whose body language suggests he is ready to pounce while you are talking.

The challenge is we process information four times quicker than a person can speak, so that in each listening minute 75% of it is idle, allowing the mind to be available to other stimuli. We need to train ourselves to pay full attention for the 60 seconds, as it is obvious the rewards are significant.

☀ PEOPLE DON'T WANT TO BE TOLD!
So, tell them stories...

Something I noticed at an early stage in my career: in relationships and business, people do not like to be dictated to. They do, however, like to be told that they know. Confused?

Let us take an example from a business situation. As a consultant, you invariably encounter initial resistance from your clients, because they'd prefer if they did not require your services in the first place. As an agent of change, the key skill required is diplomacy.

Giving advice.

The wrong way:
"You really need to be more aggressive in the marketplace."

The right way:
"You know yourself how important it is to be aggressive out there in the marketplace."

The addition of those four words "as you know yourself" changes the whole atmosphere and endears you to the client.

Storytelling.
If you want to get your message across, avoid their conscious filtering system. Tell them stories. They can't resist. People love and remember stories.

When I'm working with a client who does not recognise the need to make a change, I tell stories about someone else who has a problem that has continued to halt his progress through life. When the person let go - changed his/her strategy - his/her life was changed forever. 'Coincidentally,' my client has the same problem.

☀ PEOPLE LOVE TO BE APPRECIATED

Positive reinforcements work, for example: "Thank you," "well done," "good job."

How this has escaped so many people for so long amazes me!

Clever Communicators:

▷ Parents: praise your child's efforts. More time should be spent encouraging, rather than highlighting, their faults or mistakes.

▷ Business owners: Your employees work for more than money. Thank them for a job well done. Say it from the heart. It is a sign of your own confidence.

▷ Partners: recognise the other person's positive contribution to your life. Remember, it doesn't need to be a birthday or an anniversary for this to happen.

▷ Trainers: if you want to motivate your team, praise their efforts. Do not scream at them from the sideline telling them how useless they are!

Anyone who contributes positively to your life, thank them. It pays to appreciate.

Finally, it is imperative that you thank your inner power for it's guidance, in whatever form that feels comfortable.

☀ **PEOPLE LOVE TO LAUGH, THEY WELCOME HUMOUR!**

so make them laugh!

☀ PEOPLE LIKE OTHERS THAT ARE LIKE THEMSELVES!

To effectively build rapport with someone, we must become like them.

What are people like? Can we make predictions based on their communication styles? Yes. They have been telling you for years how to communicate with them, but you may have missed it. Just like the psychologist who asks his patient "how do you feel" after the patient has declared "I keep seeing pictures in my mind."

People's communication styles fall into one of three categories. They may use all three, but it will be obvious they have a preference for one or the other.

▷ 1. Visual   ▷ 2. Auditory   ▷ 3. Kinesthetic

When they fall into one of these categories, it becomes easier to predict much about, for example, the words they speak; their body language; eye movement, etc. Referring back to our original advice, i.e. to walk in the other person's shoes: when you have identified their preferred style, the idea is to mirror their strategy.

1. "Visual" Person.

Communication style:
Invariably their movements will be quick and sharp; palms pointing down; style animated; very speedy delivery. You'll notice they look up quite a lot. They breathe high up in the rib cage; their appearance is neat.

Eye Movement:
Frequently looking up to the left as they recall images they've seen before (VR), or looking up to the right hand side when they are imagining (VI).

Words:
When visuals process information they will want to *look* at the information, they'll want the ideas *shown* to them on paper. They want to know "your *vision* for the future." They are intimately interested in the *full picture*.
See what I mean!

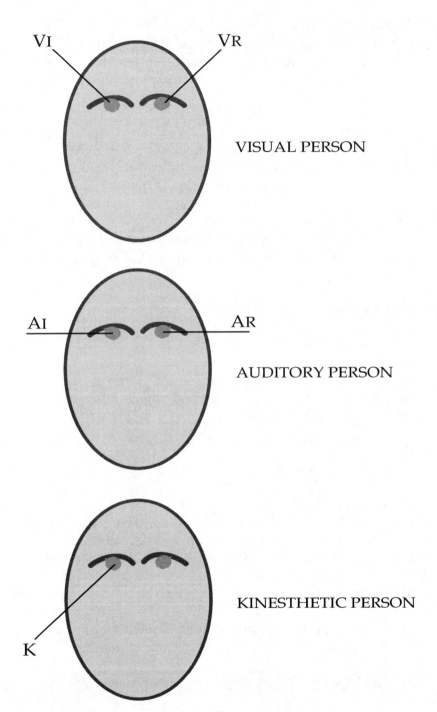

VI   VR

VISUAL PERSON

AI   AR

AUDITORY PERSON

KINESTHETIC PERSON

K

2 "Auditory" Person.

Communication style:
Voice projection: melodic and varied. They tend to touch or stroke their face a lot. Good clear enunciation. Tend to talk to themselves.

Eye Movement:
You will notice that their eyes move to the left or right, remembering a sound that has been heard before (AR), or imagining something not heard before (AI).

Words:
They'll probably want to *talk* things over; they'll expect that "you'll give them a *hearing*"; they want you to *tell them about the project.*

Does that ring a bell with you?

3 "Kinesthetic" Person.

Communication style:
Slow motion; totally different to "visuals". Voice much... slower! Expect to hear a few sighs and mmms... Breathing tends to be very full.

Eye movement:
Continually looking down to their right.

Words:
These people just can't *grasp* what you are saying; they'll need to get a *handle* on it, so they can *lay* their cards on the table; they want to have a firm *grip* on the subject, and need *concrete* examples.
It's got to feel right!

Most people will use all three styles, but it will be obvious that they have a definite preference for one or another.

You have the map: what's next?

TECHNIQUES TO BUILD BETTER RELATIONSHIPS.

Accepting that "people like others that are like themselves," to build better relationships we need to:

1 Mirror

2 Lead

1 MIRRORING.

Mirroring very simply means matching someone else's behaviour.

As Time Magazine reported on November 4th 1996:

*"Clinton went around the country, mirroring voter's every hope and hunger saying I'm just like you. Dole went looking for himself asking "are you like me?"...*surprising outcome!!

To get the chemistry right - to create those favourable first impressions - it is not essential to mirror every single aspect of the person's behaviour. To mirror doesn't mean you immediately adopt the same posture. For example, what could be seen as mimicking will cause a complete breakdown in the relationship. Instead, slowly and eloquently approximate the posture.

How do we mirror peoples behaviour?

▷ **Mirror body language.**

Many people unconsciously mirror body language.
What can be mirrored: Posture, breathing pattern, style of clothing and eye contact.

Body Language:
One day I visited a mushroom grower's farm. It was immediately apparent that the owner was a doer, not a talker! He was covered with soil from head to toe. I was dressed in a designer suit and realised that my own dress sense was a little out of place. Yes, I thought: people like others that are like themselves. In my customer's mind the most likely scenario was: "I am certainly not like him." Furthermore, I speculated that this guy was probably thinking: "this fellow never did a days work in his life." Immediately, in an attempt to address the situation, after shaking hands I asked him "is it OK if I took off my jacket, suits are not exactly my style." "No problem," he replied. After listening to him for a few moments, I decided, subconsciously, on the following plan: to speak in a more user-friendly, more accessible language; to listen with my eyes and ears and repeat what he says later on in the communication and finally to mirror his posture. We got on just fine.

In communication don't forget: *everything counts.*

▷ **Mirror Voice Projection.**

Voice Projection:
Mirror, not mimic, speed of delivery and volume.

Competency in this will ensure much better results from telephone communication. Using this medium, 75% of our decision on whether we like the person or not is down to voice projection and 25% to use of words.

Example:
Being a visual, I speak quickly. Whenever I am in conversation with a person who speaks slowly, my projection becomes much more deliberate. I have no doubt it helps to build rapport. Note, I am not suggesting you mimic people, that is too obvious. People will resent this type of strategy and if you have to change your pitch it should be gradual, not 150mph to 50mph in 2 seconds. If you do not realise how important this is, try talking at 150mph to a kinesthetic - who talks at 30mph - and build rapport. It will not be easy.

A friend of mine was going for a job she really wanted. Her background included 4 to 5 years on-the-job experience and a more than sufficient academic background. Unfortunately, on the three previous occasions she was unsuccessful in her efforts to secure a permanent job. A very confident pleasant woman, she spoke in a rather dictatorial voice. Without further analysis, I worked on toning down her voice projection. I advised her that, if by chance the person or interview panel spoke like dictators, by all means revert to her original style. The next job she went for, she was successful.

▷ Mirror Words.

Use similar vocabulary.

The psychologist friend we met at the start of this section, who was programmed to ask how the patient feels, would have mirrored his client by asking "OK, so what are you seeing?" Even more clever, before the patient opens his mouth after noting that the client was doing a lot of looking up at the ceiling, the psychologist would enquire: "how do you see it?"

The teacher who was having difficulty showing Johnny where Ireland was on the map - he couldn't *grasp* it - would bring a world globe down to the table and get him to *point* where Ireland was. Let him get a *handle* on it.

Johnny, who was madly in love with "**Auditory** Anne" should not persevere in giving her roses, but should *tell* her how much he loves her. As an aside, have you ever gone out with a partner who wanted presents; who wanted to go places to see things; who never seemed to react when you whispered those famous words, "I love you?"

Or have you ever been in the situation where you have totally turned off the person who was dressed immaculately the day you met but now goes around looking like a slob?

At a simple level, make sure your vocabulary doesn't send a subtle message to the recipient that he is stupid! The last thing a softly-spoken customer (one who delivers his message acknowledging the KISS principle: keep it short and simple) wants, is to have to listen to someone who has just swallowed the Oxford Dictionary. I have often seen this happen. The message is: **KISS** - **Keep It Simple Stupid!**

All these strategies are designed so people begin to believe you are just like them. When this happens you built rapport.

Finally, it is time to lead.

When you are like them and you have got their trust, you can now lead them on to a new strategy, a new level of thinking, with no resistance. The problem with most poor communicators is that they try to impose their will before they have built rapport with the person. It just doesn't work.

Conclusion

The recurring theme of the importance of becoming aware is especially relevant to building rapport. The master skill is made easier when you open your eyes and listen, because, as we have discovered, people are predictable.

The perfect match!

A: Matching Exercise.
Objective: To illustrate what happens when people in discussions are like each other, (similar body language; voice projection; words).

We need three participants: one to observe and two active participants. The two agree on a subject about which they share similar views. The third person observes the interaction, jotting down his observations under the following headings:

Body Language: Postures similar? Check arms, leg positions etc.
Voice Projection: Volume similar? Does it change? What happens with the other person when one changes style?
Use of Words: similar vocabulary?

Let the discussion begin. The exercise should last for no more than 15 minutes.

Post mortem.
Initially, the observer should find out how each participant felt about the communication.
Then, the observer should say what is left unsaid by the participants on reviewing the exercise.

B: Mismatching Exercises.
Objective: To show what happens when you mismatch a person's body language or voice, while simultaneously agreeing with what they say.

(i) Now get the two participants to agree on another subject about which they share similar views. This time get one to mismatch completely (adopt different body language, voice projection) to the other person.

The mismatchers may look away, have a different posture, speak quicker or slower than the other person, but at all times their words show they are in agreement.

The observer jots down his/her observations under similar headings to exercise A.

How does each of the participants feel now? Did the observer notice anything interesting when one of the participants was mismatching? Did the other person start to mirror them?

Discuss.

OR

(ii) Get the participants to agree on a topic for discussion about which they have different views. This time they have to mirror the other person while disagreeing.

What did the observer notice this time? How did the participants feel after this exercise?

What did they learn from each experiment? Compare and contrast A and B from a communications perspective.

Possible observations

1: The participants perform an intimate mirroring act. They may be sitting in similar postures. Check it out (arms folded, legs crossed, hands together). In addition, their delivery (voice projection) may be more similar at the end of the process than at the start.

2: The participants will find it very awkward to agree while mismatching simultaneously. Conversation will likely be patchy; unclear; they probably would have found it easier to argue; no flow.

3: Participants will find it difficult not to try to mirror.

ACTION 24

Voice Power

Objective: An appreciation of one of your greatest assets: your voice.

Tape your voice and play it back. Remember, the voice you hear when you are speaking is not the voice we hear when we are listening! Analyse the following: the tone, volume and speed. Happy? Remember, no matter when you are communicating, if you speak in a monotonous voice you induce fatigue. When the message is cold the answer will be cold.

ACTION ■ 25

Look me in the eye and I'll tell you who you are.

Objective: To show how predictable people are. This fun exercise makes you more aware of the fact that in communication everything counts. If someone continues to look up to the left while they are speaking to you, it is advisable you speak in 'visual' terms to them!

Eye Movements!
Note eye movements for the following questions:

▷ What colour was your fourth last car?
▷ What colour was your maths book in Leaving Cert.?
▷ Imagine going out on a date with _____
▷ Which sound do you prefer: door bell or alarm clock?
▷ What would it feel like to walk in the snow in your bare feet?
▷ Tell yourself "I am a champion" over and over again.
▷ How would you feel if a car ran over your foot?

Communication Channels:

Body Language: The way we walk; head up/down; shoulders back/slumped; weak/strong handshake; hand movements; good/poor eye contact; slumped/upright posture; ability/inability to smile.
Picture the following: at the end of the day, a job-hunter enters the interview room with a smile on his/her face, and automatically the atmosphere is recharged. It takes 72 muscles to frown and only 14 to smile.

Voice projection: Texture, pitch, tone, volume.

Words: Vocabulary.

What have you learned?

How are you going to benefit from this new knowledge?

7

CHOOSING WHO YOU LISTEN TO

"If you wish to know the road up the mountain, you must ask the man who goes back and forth on it" - Japanese Zenrin.

In 1990, I left England to set up a marketing consultancy business in my home town in Ireland. One weekend, I bumped into an associate of mine whose mental programming had always eliminated him as a possible contributor to my journey through life. If the sun was cracking the rocks outside, he was the type of chap that would invariably question how long it would last.

Deeply inquisitive by nature, he wanted to know specifically what I intended doing in my business. After several vague answers and an intimate cross-examination period, I told him my vision of the future. He declared: "that will never work in this country, it has been tried before." My reply was sharp and better left unrepeated. Luckily, his comments had no impact whatsoever on my self-belief, my passion, my vision, because as he spoke, I continually ran this question in my mind: "what have you done in that area in your life?" The answer was "nothing," so his comments were irrelevant.

When I reflect on this story, it somewhat saddens me. Many people listen to people like this, never analysing the source and subsequently desist from following their desired path through life. Many people do not realise that some are likely to be upset by your energy. They would prefer the sad story.

I use the same strategy to this day whenever someone volunteers advice on any aspect of my life. I play the tape over and over again in my subconscious. Very simply, if the person hasn't succeeded in that particular context, their advice doesn't pass the conscious filtering system. If, on the other hand, this person has been there, done that, my ears are open - wide open.

CHOOSING WHO YOU LISTEN TO IS THE CRITICAL STRATEGY IN LIFE.

Why?

One commentator's research suggested that for every *positive* a person gets, they receive eight *negatives*. Let us assume that the person interprets all these incoming messages as the truth. Bear in mind that it is the interpretation that counts. What type of person do you expect at the end of the process: a positive, vibrant, energetic human being? I doubt it.

In a study my company conducted with 1,000 students, the majority said they received more criticism than praise in their life. At the end of this type of moulding process, what can you expect from a cat, but a kitten! To highlight the results of this type of conditioning, ask kids to write five good things about themselves. Get them to follow this by writing five bad things. Kids usually have a problem with the five good things, no problem with twenty bad ones!

To get the balance right, we need to monitor what gets written on our inner program, to filter everything at source.

WHO SHOULD YOU LISTEN TO?

It is crucial not to generalise. You can't assume any source is a good source. You must judge everyone on their individual merits. Most people do the best they can with the knowledge they possess. Sometimes however, with the best will in the world, they are ill-informed, so their advice, if accepted, can have detrimental effects on a person's psychology.

"Keep away from people who try to belittle your ambitions. Small people always do that but the really great make you feel

that you too can become great" - Mark Twain.

Examples:

Partners.
"No man is an island." Very few have the exclusive on all the knowledge in the universe, consequently your partner will be an excellent source for some things; for others they won't have the necessary resources.

Furthermore, if you are, as we will discuss in chapter 8, in a 1+1=3 relationship, where both are independent people but together they are better, your partner will usually be constructive. However, if you are suffering in an unbalanced relationship where 1+1=1 or 1+1=0, the likelihood is your partner may resent your striving for a better life.

As an aside, oftentimes we put unfair pressure on a relationship by expecting our partner to have all the answers.

Parents.
Most parents want the best for their children.

Invariably they do the best they can with the knowledge they have. But sometimes, no matter how they try, they too can cause damage. *"Don't worry, not everybody is good at maths."* This is a comment aired in the home-place that will resonate with many people. The parent may be trying to console the child, but instead they may have imprinted in the child's subconscious: *"can't be good at everything,"* or, worse still *"anything."*

It is interesting to note that in one study, 90% of prisoners had been told repeatedly by their parents *"someday you are going to end up in jail."*

In another study*, they found that there was a substantially higher level of unemployment among school leavers whose fathers were unemployed (32%), as compared with 14% of all school leavers. Emulating the wrong person?

Parents are usually role models, as was my experience. The study referred to above also showed that children's participation in further studies whose fathers belong to professional or employer/manager categories is markedly higher than that for other categories. It is my belief that parents can build a foundation that no other influencer can destroy (see chapter 6).

Teachers/School System.

The current school system restricts the teacher's scope in the classroom. Society has dictated that grades make the man/woman! Thus, the emphasis on linguistic intelligence (the stuff that makes grades) in the classroom is at the expense of interpersonal (the ability to get on with others) and intrapersonal intelligence (the ability to know oneself, to motivate oneself). As mentioned earlier, the latter are the two most well-paid intelligences in the world. So the system churns out many 'intelligent' people who cannot communicate to save their lives, who experience pain in the real world, and furthermore leaves thousands of students who didn't make the grade feeling inadequate and stupid.

Unlike playschool, where the child's learning experience is rich and varied, the school system adopts a style suited to the visuals and auditories (people whose preferences are to absorb information by seeing it or listening to someone talk about it).

Meanwhile, for the kinesthetic (those who like to feel/handle things), their learning style is deemed redundant. As they can't absorb information in the current structure they too are deemed remedial. Another failure mentality is born. We are well aware of the many people who didn't make the grade, yet were very, very successful in life. Closer to home, we all know people who lead very fulfilling lives; enjoy excellent relationships; enjoy their job; make a serious contribution to the community. Many of these also didn't make the grade, so who's fooling who?

*Study source: The Economic Status of School Leavers 1993-1995, ESRI.

On the other hand, school has managed to rescue some children from the "I can't do" mentality which has been programmed in their homes.

Furthermore, some teachers put everything they've got on the line for their students. Many 'die' the night before the exam results, fearing any negative outcome for their adopted family. This commitment can only have a positive effect on the child.

Media.
People are being fed a diet of dangerous ideals from the media. *"This is the way you should look to be happy."* For many who tune in to these ideals, their self-esteem suffers from the surreal comparison. In a study completed by students at Gorey Community College in County Wexford, out of 650 people interviewed (500 girls and 150 boys), 60% of girls said the images portrayed in the media gave them a negative self-image. Worse still, 15% felt they had to emulate the 'models:' those with beautiful figures, many of whom are extremely unhappy. Furthermore, 60% of the sample had gone on a strict diet. Their goal: attain model shape status; to look like 'models.' They probably believed this new shape would solve all their problems.

Again, the media can be a vital and important source of information.

Friends.
As those difficult teenage years approach, in most cases our friends become our dominant influence, replacing our parents. "Tell me your company and I'll tell you who you are." Your choice of friends and subsequent reference group in life is probably the single most critical decision that you face. Your pursuit of personal happiness will be greatly assisted by your association with like-minded people. Choose the right group and they will propel you to success and happiness. Choose the wrong group, they will hold you back. As people like others that are like themselves, for a positive person to survive in a negative group (a fate worse then death for some people) will involve a serious change in strategy, otherwise they risk being expelled.

Reflection
Judge advisors on their own individual merits. Just because they are your partners, parents, teachers, friends, or the 'in' media does not mean they are right. You must benchmark people who have proved their competency in that particular context. Talk to the best

professionals in their chosen field. Talk to someone who has an excellent relationship if you need advice on relationships. Talk to the best fitness instructors if you want to get fit (not a couch potato!). Very simply, model off excellence.

My story continues:

In 1990, I made a conscious decision to bounce my ideas off a select group of people. These people enjoyed an excellent reputation in the training industry. Any ideas I had were shared with my expert focus group. Sometimes they rejected the ideas and I would invariably reconsider my position. Sometimes they endorsed them, and I went full steam ahead. In addition to being excellent at their jobs, they were well-balanced individuals. I critically analysed everything they did, what books they read; what courses they attended; listened to their recommendations; reviewed the communication strategies they used and identified their core beliefs about life. This really kicked off my journey. I began to learn for the first time who were the top trainers in the world. I started to read their books and attend their lectures.

Over the following seven years, I attended courses conducted by the top trainers in the world. My investment was huge, but the rewards made it worthwhile. I found that I had outgrown my initial focus group, so it was time to move on if I wanted my business to progress.

I now refer my ideas to a new group which consists of top consultants in Australia, America and Ireland. It is inevitable that this group will propel me to greater heights.

Finally, I offer unparalleled access to my new learning to the people that started me on this exciting journey. Remember the best way to learn is to teach others.

The strategy involves:

▷ Seeking out the best people in that particular discipline.
▷ Airing your ideas and being willing to accept their verdict: positive or negative.
▷ Analysing everything they do. What can you learn from them? Remember, you are never going to live long enough to make all the mistakes that have been made in the world to

date.

▷ Keeping going until you feel that your advisory group can bring you no further. At this stage it is important you seek out new mentors who can assist you in your passage.

As a footnote, it has been my experience, indeed the experience of many, that the most brilliant people are invariably the most accessible; the most willing to impart knowledge. The converse is also true: the least approachable were those who "didn't make the grade." Ironic? Yes.

"Life's most persistent and urgent question, what are you doing for others?" Martin Luther King.

Finally, it is necessary that you reward your review panel for their help: never take them for granted. Give them something for all that you have received. Every one of my relationships is based around this reciprocal arrangement. It is the way it should be: both growing together.

An example from the 'underdeveloped' world:

High in the Andes there exists a tribe of Indians who have not had any interaction with the developed world. On meeting a member of the tribe for the first time, one of them sets a challenge. Let's assume it is a race: a two-mile race through the forest. This underdeveloped society demands that the victor of the race coaches the vanquished, until he attains an equivalent competency. In return the vanquished must teach the victor a new skill in another discipline. Think about it: a society growing together. Our developed world has managed to polarise society. Who is developed?

Remember, "a candle loses nothing lighting another."

As I have progressed through life, I realise that phenomenal personal power is available to everyone as long as our motivation is to add value to this planet. All we have got to do is tune in and we will be shown the way.

Many of my decisions are now based on intuition. If I feel drawn to some place, I go there; if not, I don't. My belief is that we have all the answers, just as the Greek philosophers asserted "the universe is in us." Just this week I had decided consciously that I would go away to a hotel and write the rest of this book. Every morning I looked at the back of the paper for inspiration from advertisements. I felt no attraction whatsoever to any of the hotels. Finally, I decided to check out what was available on the Aran Islands. I contacted a hotel there who promised to send out a brochure but it never came. I decided to stay put. At home that night (remember I wasn't supposed to be there), I got a phone call from one of the top consultants in Ireland, regarding a very high-profile contract. The following day, I got a call from my friend from Australia (two of his stories appear in this book). Finally I sat down on Saturday morning with my colleague Margaret, who cross-examined me on my manuscript. It was a fantastic learning experience. Bottom line: the universe had intervened: I wasn't supposed to go!

"If I have seen farther than most men it is because I stood on the shoulders of greats" Isaac Newton.

Conclusion

Your choice of reference group is one of the most critical decisions you will make in life. Judge each member of this group on their own individual merits. You cannot assume that just because they are your friends - your partner - your teachers - your parents - that they should be listened to.

When you select your mentors, adopt a give and take approach. As we mentioned in the last chapter, people love to be appreciated, so thank them for their help in an appropriate fashion. Never, **ever**, take them for granted.

When the time is right seek out a new group that can bring you to the next level. Simultaneously you should be helping your former mentors to get to your new level. Always remember the best way to learn is by teaching others.

ACTION 26

Listening to those who know.

Objective: To highlight the mould-makers in your life; after reviewing their input, to be in a position to prime yourself for more constructive contribution from people in the future. Surrounding yourself with people who can give you constructive feedback will change your life forever. The people you love the most may be your worst advisors.

▷ List all the major influencers in your life; the people who have moulded you into what you are.

▷ For each of them write down what you like most about them.

▷ Follow this by describing what you dislike about them. What are your conclusions? What do you need to do? Who should you listen to?

ACTION 27

Modelling off excellence

Objective: Imprinting on your subconscious the type of person you desire to be.

Draw a caricature of the person you most admire. List the desired attributes that person possesses and pin it up on your study wall.

ACTION 28

Should I listen or not?

Objective: To reject garbage on first hearing.

Next time someone is volunteering information on some aspect of your life, run the 'tape': "what have you done in that area in your life?" No history - no impact!

ACTION 29

Words, what do they mean?

Objective: To clarify peoples comments/suggestions before accepting them as realistic.

Challenge Those Words!
When someone says things are not possible, it usually reflects

their own thinking. Grab a colleague. In five minutes tell them all about yourself.

You'll probably notice that when you spoke, as we all do, you changed information, you deleted information and you made generalisations. Accepting this, and realising the effect people's words have on your psychology, it is essential that you clarify the meaning of the person's communication, both for yourself and for the other person.

Your enquiry will yield better and more accurate information. Sometimes the message intended isn't the same as the initial message received.

Source Analysis!
               How to respond.

Statement: *It won't work.*
               (An example of a sweeping generalisation)

Questioning strategy:

"It won't work?"
               (Say using a 'shocked' voice projection)

"It won't work for anybody?"

"Have you ever met anybody that it *did* work for?"

"How do you know?"

The answers to any of these questions will clarify the person's statement. Then you decide whether or not to accept it.

Whenever you hear *always, everybody, nobody* type statements, (generalisations), clarify immediately. Bottom line: make sure what you accept as the truth is the **real** truth.

ACTION ▦ 30

Give!

The challenge: Give a little!

A little gift!

▷ No matter who you visit in the future, commit yourself to leaving the person or group with a gift, tangible or intangible.
▷ If you have a partner, give a gift at an unexpected time.
▷ In your job, give your employer or your client more than is expected. No matter what client I am working with, an attempt is made to give more than what was in my original brief. At all training sessions I conduct, business people are asked if they have exceeded their customers expectations (e.g. referring business to them). This is incredibly powerful strategy.
▷ Help somebody that you know to achieve their goals (real challenge: try helping your competition!).

Reflection for those who tried:
▷ Did you find it difficult? Why? Remember, being addicted to material things is the same as being addicted to drink, drugs or work. What have you learned about yourself? More importantly, what can you do to improve this situation?
▷ Did you find that you improved your own knowledge as a result? The best way to learn is to teach what you know.
▷ Did you notice a series of positive circumstances (a new teacher appearing or new intuitions happening in your life)? How did you interpret this? (Payback?)

"Blessed are those who give without remembering and take without forgetting" - Elizabeth Bibesco.

What have you learned?

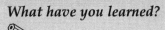

How are you going to benefit from this new knowledge?

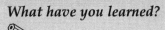

8

TO LOVE YOURSELF, THE START OF GREAT RELATIONSHIPS

The book so far has focused on self-empowerment: equipping you with the necessary techniques to make your passage through life a more fulfilling one. By using some of these exercises, you will begin to realise just how powerful you are. This new belief will have a dramatic positive effect on your self-esteem. How critical your levels of self-esteem are in the context of building relationships cannot be overemphasised.

The bottom line is simple: if you don't love yourself you will find it hard to give out love either to your children or your partner. Loving yourself is not a selfish desire: it is a prerequisite for successful relationships.

In this chapter, two of the more typical type relationships we encounter in our lifetime are reviewed.

BOY MEETS GIRL!

WHAT IS LOVE?

1 + 1 = 3...synergy!

People grow together in a relationship. Apart, they are instruments each capable of playing beautiful tunes. Together they are a symphony. They are committed to each individual's growth within the relationship; they both know what they want out of the relationship; they are best friends; totally undisturbed and secure in the relationship. They accept each other as they are. It involves two people who listen to their hearts, not their head.

WHAT IS NOT LOVE?

Warning signs:
1 + 1 = 1, or worse still 1 + 1 = 0.

☀ Misleading beliefs about a relationship.

▷ It will be OK, they will change!
Sorry, but they will not change: take them as they are or leave. That is why the student/teacher relationship, where one tries to mould the other into their likeness, never works! Suddenly one starts to lose his/her identity in the relationship. Sooner or later resentment will come to the surface. Ironically, if you get married in a Catholic Church, you symbolically lose your identify on the day! Two candles at the start of the mass become one after you get married. I was recently informed that one far-seeing American priest decided to light both individual candles and also the unity candle.
1 + 1 = 3 - the way it should be.

▷ They will solve my problems
If Mary is not all there, Johnny is not going to make her complete.

▷ Relationships can make you happy!
As one of my students put it "extra happy, yes; happy, no". Happiness, like love, is who you are, it is not a relationship. Only you can make yourself happy.

☀ Motivation for a relationship does not stand up.

▷ It is time to settle down.
"I have to (because of prevailing circumstances)." "I might never get anybody better." "I don't want to hurt them". None of these stand up and certainly don't inspire much confidence that this will be a fulfilling relationship. Even worse, it sounds like the next generation is about to suffer.

☀ Clinging on rather than letting go.
In all secure relationships the doors are open.

☀ **Not interested in your interests.**
A good common interest is a good common bond.

☀ **You are not listening.**

"If you ever have an intuitive inner knowing, don't accept anyone else's opinion - pursue yours" - Bernie Siegal.

How many know in their heart that their relationship has not got what it takes, but persist? How many people are being told by their "true friends" that something's up, but they won't listen? How many people take no account of a series of apparent coincidences which are directing them away from the relationship? It is bizarre: they know, but they don't want to know.

☀ **You are not talking from the heart.**
This is a particular problem some men have: you ask them to describe their feelings, they speak from the head, not the heart. At a similar level, not being able to talk about anything at any level is an even bigger problem.

☀ **Criteria for selection are weak** (particularly relevant when you are younger.).

"Beauty doesn't make the pot boil" - Irish Proverb.

☀ **The relationship is not fun.**
For me, this is the all-embracing bottom line. The tragedy is that some people are not having fun. They suffer so much in a certain relationship that they generalise this is true for all relationships. *Only suffering will come my way.*

What Can You Do?

1 Work on yourself. Remember, love is who you are, not a relationship. Believe in yourself. Expect to attract your ideal soulmate into your life. You deserve it.

2 When the choice is between something you want and something you want more, go for the latter.

ACTION ◪ 31

Taking them as they are.

Objective: Full disclosure. Get all problems out in the open before lift-off.

Most people carry some degree of emotional baggage into a relationship (some more then others). Before critical decisions are made such as marriage, engagement or moving in together, it is imperative that all such problems are aired and accepted by both partners. For the relationship to work it requires full disclosure from both partners with all secrets out in the open. The stuff they were afraid to speak about in the past: get it out!

Why?
Many relationships fail because this baggage turns up on life's conveyor belt sooner or later and one partner cannot accept it. At this stage the breakdown is likely to hurt more people than just two.

If it is love, the relationship will transcend such obstacles. You *must* be able to comfortably discuss anything with your partner.

What do you want?

Objective: To ensure that both partners are on the same wavelength.

Step 1: Together with your intended - someone with whom you have decided to spend the rest of your life - with or without the help of a close friend (sometimes their help is imperative because they can see), write down what you want out of life/what you expect out of a relationship. **BE SELFISH, DEMAND WHAT YOU WANT UP FRONT!** Being selfish in this context is not necessarily a negative thing. What you want to work at. How many kids? Where will they go to school? What type of school will they attend? Where do you want to live? How many holidays a year? What type of house? How much time do you want alone with your partner? Absolutely everything. The full script.

Step 2: Compare notes: is there common ground? She is a career woman, he wants a housewife. What are you going to do about that?

We know that we cannot predict what is going to happen throughout life. We also know that even if you complete these exercises, a fairytale is not guaranteed. It does mean, however, that both partners are going into the relationship with their eyes open.

Recently I heard a perfect example of what happens as a result of the blindness we develop in a relationship:

My friend Val noticed the following cartoon one day in a paper. Two people are sitting at the breakfast table, one reading the paper, the other devouring his cereal. Husband looks out from the side of the paper, asks the wife to pass the sugar. The wife looks up vacantly and asks:"who are you?" Val could really identify with the story. She had been married to her husband for quite some time. After the initial 'champagne reception' welcoming the beginning of any relationship, followed by the 'distraction' of the kids who had grown up and left the family home, she realised that she was the woman in the cartoon. After all these years she realised there had never been a relationship in the first place: she didn't know her husband.

Many people have suffered a similar fate to Val. One woman eloquently put it in the following fashion: "it was screaming at both of us before we got married, but we didn't want to see or listen, we were in love." We've got to listen to our intuitions and accept short-term pain for long-term pleasure.

My directive is simple, yet controversial...hold out for the fairytale.

There are two very important reasons for saying this:

1. You deserve to be happy!

2. Your decision has a huge knock-on effect on the generations to come.

Kids are very perceptive. They subscribe to the "I'll do as my parents do, rather than say" theory. So, if they notice a lack of love between their parents, several possible disastrous conclusions can be reached:

They may start to believe, rightly or wrongly (its their *interpretation* that counts): "It is my fault, I do not deserve love." Or: "this is the way it should be." To show love is wrong: "love hurts."

With this type of belief structure this person will always find it difficult to go for promotions or jobs. "I don't deserve it." They will find it even more difficult to have a relationship, or indeed extract themselves from a poor one. Even worse, they will have great difficulty showing unconditional love to their children (so it goes on and on and on. Generations suffer).

This is why I believe relationships are the key to our future.

FAMILY MATTERS

At this stage in my career, I have addressed several thousand parents on their potential influence on the next generation. I have observed a remarkable - or maybe not that remarkable - pattern emerging. After having the students for three sessions, I could predict with 85% accuracy how many parents would turn up at a parents' night. Indeed I remember one night arriving at a hall where 60 chairs had been left out. I indicated to the teacher a crowd of 18 people was a more likely attendance. He disagreed. 19 turned up. In 95%+ of all groups I have addressed, the same pattern emerged. Furthermore, the first people to speak after the presentation were the bubbly kids' parents! My calculations were based on noting the kids' attitude in class; their own self-respect, etc. Those who were willing to learn, those that had positive expectations, their bubbly, energetic parents invariably attended.

The students who had low self-esteem and limited expectations, who wanted attention and were generally disruptive? Their parents rarely ventured.

Early Start!

It comes as no surprise to me that many experts believe that 80% of a child's personality is developed by the age of five. The majority of this time is spent with parents or nannies. When you couple this with a lack of analytical ability during those years (anything they see they process as fact/reality), it becomes obvious why many of us become *"Mac an dhaidi"*: the son of my father.

I find this information to be very encouraging, because it was my belief up to then that friends were the most dominant influence in a child's life. I agree that they are an influence but I believe if the right foundation is in place the structure will survive.

Parents can make them before friends can break them. That's my belief.

Getting the best out of your children:

▷ Start with yourself (I'm becoming predictable). Kids can sense if there's a problem at home. Develop yourself. The more love you have for yourself, the more you can dish out to your children.

▷ 0 - 5 years, critical time. Make sure you spend as much time with your children as possible. Some people would argue that, years ago, when the extended family was together, kids got more time and attention. They subsequently developed into stronger personalities. Now, we are rapidly developing into the 'nanny culture' with very little developmental input from parents. This is not ideal. Indeed, I think the role of the home parent (as one woman called it the 'domestic engineer's role) should be recognised in some way by the state. Remember, future generations are in their hands. **One moment can irreparably damage a child's life.** Remember again, from 0 - 5 kids have no analytical ability, so everything they see they process as reality. If parents fight, "its my fault;" "I don't deserve love." Disastrous thought pattern installed.

▷ Be *"do as I do"* parents, not *"do as I say"*. Kids are clever. Telling your children they shouldn't smoke or drink while you freely indulge just doesn't work!

▷ Celebrate failures and mistakes with them. They will realise that failure is acceptable; a part of the process. Make sure when they are reflecting on their childhood they don't remember you as the person who only got involved when someone needed to be disciplined and nothing else!

▷ Give them responsibility; involve them in decisions; listen to their opinions; empower them where appropriate. Certainly do not disempower. Small things like letting them take care of their football gear, their room, or making their bed are useful self-esteem builders.

▷ Never *Ass-u-Me*; (because it makes an *ass* out of *u* and *me!*) show them they are loved unconditionally. At no stage let them think that your love for them is dependent on a, b, c, d. Cuddles and kisses as well as positive words are recommended. Several studies have shown that a special touch can make the difference.
One study, conducted by the University of Miami, showed that, in a sample of two groups of premature babies, the ones stroked 3 times a day for 10 minutes through an opening in the crib gained on average 49% more weight per day than a group given the same formula diet but no cuddles.

▷ Instil patterns like *"I can do it;" "It's OK to fail;" "I am loved unconditionally;" "I am responsible;" I am good with people;" "I can make a difference."*

▷ A common mistake is to impose your will and your desires on the child. Their goal must be something they want, not what you want. Give a life! Do not try to live your life through them. Too often we meet pushy parents who are not interested in their children's successes for their children's sake, but more for their own public relations campaign.

▷ Continue a winning strategy. You spend the first few years encouraging them to talk, the next few, sometimes, telling them to shut up. Revert to the winning strategy.

▷ When administering criticism, focus on the activity, not the person. Focus on the future, not the past. More importantly, describe negative behaviour using temporary language:

Don't say - *"Mary you are always messing up."*
Do say - *"I know you aren't always messing...but..!"* Conversely,
use permanent language when you are describing positive
behaviour. *"Yes, you are a very confident young woman."*

Conclusion

"Love your neighbour as yourself." It does not say *"love your
neighbour more than yourself."* When you love yourself, wonderful
things start to happen. Sooner or later, you attract the type of
partner you want into your life, as your confidence allows you to
wait. You can expect happier, healthier children who will thrive on
your love. You can expect a more fulfilling journey through life.

ACTION 33

It is on the tree!

Objective: To notice any recurring themes.

Complete the family chart. Go back as far as you can. Include
in it how many children your relations had; any addictions;
any diseases; what age they died; everything! Do you notice
any patterns emerging? Are you looking to marry your
mother/father?

What have you learned?

How are you going to benefit from this new knowledge?

9
ALL GREAT ACHIEVEMENTS START WITH ONE SMALL STEP

"So much sadness in the world...so little action."

Sad stories: "I'm deeply unhappy in my relationship;" "I detest my job with a passion;" "I'm gonna do...when I have the time." Same old sad stories. Only one solution: take action. Taking action at any level, even one small step, will change your life forever.

In 1983, Fintan got the news "it is not looking good; this could be terminal" the diagnosis - a brain haemorrhage. In the hospital, he was informed that he had a 40/60 chance of survival. The operation didn't go according to plan. For three minutes Fintan was clinically dead. After eleven hours, he was brought back to his bed. For the following five days he lay there in a coma, his family by his bedside. After regaining consciousness, to his family's relief, he spent 3 or 4 weeks convalescing. Honouring his wishes, he was transferred to his local hospital in Letterkenny.

Hour after hour he sat there feeling (in his own words) "lovely and sorry for myself; life was cruel; what's the point; I never have any luck." One day his damaging thought pattern was interrupted by a voice calling his name. At the top of the ward was a physiotherapist coming towards him." Some assistance for me," Fintan hoped.

He acknowledged the lady, who retorted, "unlucky soul! What are you doing here. Let's be having you." Fintan looked at her quizzically, commenting "I need help." "No you don't! Get up by yourself," she replied. So, using the curtains around the bed as support, he pulled himself out. Bang! Down came the curtains and railings. Fintan went tumbling to the ground. Surely she's going to help me now. No joy. It was time to take action; to take responsibility again.

He started to crawl towards the chair. As he reached it he was helped up by the lady. Fintan recognised this moment as the defining moment in his life. He realised there was no point in waiting for the world to solve your problems - you had to take responsibility yourself. Look what can happen when you start taking action - when you start believing - when you move outside your comfort zone. Step by step, Fintan got back to work.

Unsatisfied with the challenge of working for others, Fintan set up his own company. He and his wife Marie are now running a successful cleaning and equipment distribution company.

ACTION 34

Time to take serious action!

☀ Write down your goals for the next year; 5 years; 10 years; 20 years.

☀ Identify your mission.

☀ Who can help you? Who can be your mentor? Commit to contacting them immediately.

☀ Commit to daily use of techniques until they become a habit - just like driving a car. Take time out to be; to listen to the power within.

☀ Be flexible: accept that negative outcomes require a change in strategy.

☀ Above all enjoy it!

The last word

If you thought you could attract a more suitable partner or sort out problems with your existing one; raise happier healthier children; have a better job; enjoy a better lifestyle by taking action; in summary, live the fairytale, be happy, would it motivate you? Well **you can,** because everything becomes possible when you take action.

__Take action, you deserve to be happy__

What have you learned?

How are you going to benefit from this new knowledge?

If you are interested in further information
on courses, tapes, or any details of our company,
contact us at:

Advanced Marketing,
3 Fee Court,
Church Street,
Longford, Ireland.

Telephone: 043-47555/47211
Fax: 043-47980
e mail: kkmark@iol.ie

BIBLIOGRAPHY

Intelligence, Multiple Perspectives: Howard Gardner, Mindy L. Kornahaber, Warren K. Wake. Harcourt Brace College Publishers.

The Celestine Prophecy, An Experimental Guide: James Redfield, Carol Adrienne. Bantam Books.

Ageless Body, Timeless Mind: Deepak Chopra. Rider, Ebury Press, Random House Publications, 20 Vauxhall Bridge Road, London SW1V 2SA.

The Tibetan Book of Living and Dying: Sogyal Rinpoche. Rider Books.

NLP, The new Technology of Achievement: Edited by Steve Andreas and Charles Faulkner. Quill William Morrow.

On Jung: Anthony Stevens. Penguin Books.

Franz Kafka, A Biography. Max Brod. Da Capo Press.

Accelerated Learning: Colin Rose.